SAFE & [barcode: D0628591]

"As our country gracefully a ... o all we can to protect the elderly—from their health, to their mind, to their finances. Once again, a man we all trust and respect has stepped forward and answered the call to help. With his simple and effective ways of explaining important concepts, legend Fran Tarkenton is doing his part to keep the elderly safe, drawing on his own successful career both on and off the football field."

> —SANJAY GUPTA, Assistant Professor of Neurosurgery at Emory University and CNN Chief Medical Correspondent

"As more and more of our citizens are reaching their senior years, it means an exploding marketplace for senior fraudsters. They are everywhere! This book is as essential to your financial safety as seat belts are in the car. Keep it handy every day!"

> —SCOTT MILLER, CEO of Core Strategy Group

"From helping us all recognize that we're potential targets to providing easily comprehensible and implementable solutions, Fran Tarkenton and Rick Gossett have provided an extremely invaluable and indispensable resource. Elder financial abuse will remain a major concern as our population ages. The tools presented here can help everyone be prepared and make them less likely to be a victim."

> —THOMAS E. PRICE, MD, former Secretary of Health and Human Services and former member of US House of Representatives

"*Safe & Secure* is both timely and astute. It addresses an insidious threat to one of the largest demographic populations in our society, one that most of us do not equate with vulnerability. Fran and Rick offer critical insights into the dehumanizing process that occurs when seniors are subjected to financial exploitation and how this often precedes psychological, physical, and even sexual abuse.

With so much of our contemporary popular culture's focus on the Millennial generation or Gen Y, it is all too easy to overlook the fact that our Traditionalist and Baby Boomer populaces are often considered soft targets for predators in our society.

Safe & Secure not only raises these issues and brings the problem of victimization into the plain light of day; it also delivers the essential tools and strategies for prevention. This is a must read for seniors but also for any of us. This generation deserves our collective esteem and respect, but more than anything, our vigilance in protecting their financial and personal security."

—ANTHONY HORTON, author and DVP of Business Development at ADP, LLC

"This book cannot be more timely or relevant to today's seniors. The importance of planning and choosing the right individual(s) to help seniors plan has become increasingly more difficult and *Safe & Secure* offers great advice! This book should be a must read for the entire family, those taking care of themselves, and those looking after seniors."

—MARK WILLIAMS, President and CEO at Brokers International

SAFE & SECURE

SAFE & SECURE

10 ESSENTIAL STEPS for SENIORS to Protect Against Financial Abuse

FRAN TARKENTON
and RICK GOSSETT

REGNERY
PUBLISHING
A Division of Salem Media Group

Regnery® is a registered trademark of Salem Communications Holding Corporation

Cataloging-in-Publication data on file with the Library of Congress

ISBN 978-1-62157-817-8
ebook ISBN 978-1-62157-842-0

Published in the United States by
Regnery Publishing
A Division of Salem Media Group
300 New Jersey Ave NW
Washington, DC 20001
www.Regnery.com

Manufactured in the United States of America

10 9 8 7 6 5 4 3 2 1

Books are available in quantity for promotional or premium use. For information on discounts and terms, please visit our website: www.Regnery.com.

CONTENTS

DISCLAIMER

This publication contains the opinions and ideas of its authors. It is intended to provide helpful and informative material on the subject matter covered. It is sold with the understanding that the author and publisher are not engaged in rendering professional services in the book. The information provided is not intended as tax, investment, or legal advice, and should not be relied on as such. If the reader requires personal assistance or advice, you are encouraged to seek tax, investment, or legal advice from an independent professional advisor. The authors are not endorsed by or affiliated with the Social Security Administration or any government agency.

The author and publisher specifically disclaim any responsibility for any liability, loss, or risk, personal or otherwise, which is incurred as a consequence, directly or indirectly, of the use and application of any of the contents of this book.

All terms mentioned in this book that are known to be or are suspected of being trademarks or service marks have been appropriately capitalized. The publisher cannot attest to the accuracy of this information. Use of a term in this book should not be regarded as affecting the validity of any trademark or service mark.

This book provides general information that is intended but not guaranteed to be correct and up-to-date information on the subjects discussed and should not be regarded as a complete analysis of these subjects. You should not rely on statements or representations made within the book or by any externally referenced sources. No party assumes liability for any loss or damage resulting from errors or omissions or reliance on or use of this material.

The author does not assume any responsibility for actions or non-actions taken by people who have read this book, and no one shall be entitled to a claim for detrimental reliance based upon any information provided or expressed herein. Your use of any information provided does not constitute any type of contractual relationship between yourself and the provider(s) of this information. The author hereby disclaims all responsibility and liability for all use of any information provided in this book. The materials here are not to be interpreted as establishing an attorney-client or any other relationship between the reader and the authors or their firm.

Although great effort has been expended to ensure that only the most meaningful resources are referenced in these pages, the author does not endorse, guarantee, or warranty the accuracy, reliability, or thoroughness of any referenced information, product, or service. Any opinions, advice, statements, services, offers, or other information or content expressed or made available by third parties are those of the author(s) or publisher(s) alone. References to other sources of information do not constitute a referral, endorsement, or recommendation of any product or service. The existence of any particular reference is simply intended to imply potential interest to the reader.

The views expressed herein are exclusively those of the author and do not represent the views of any other person or any organization with which the author is or may be associated.

THE CRIME OF THE TWENTY-FIRST CENTURY— "ELDER FINANCIAL ABUSE"

THE CRIME OF THE TWENTY-FIRST CENTURY— "ELDER FINANCIAL ABUSE"

"With good reason, financial elder abuse has been characterized by some experts as 'the crime of the twenty-first century.'"

—J.F. Wasik[1]

I don't know about you, but we are tired of hearing about elderly individuals and couples being financially abused. Many have lost thousands of dollars or been left destitute. Worse yet, many are suffering not just financial abuse, but related mental, emotional, and physical, and sometimes even sexual abuse at the hands of the perpetrators.

7

OUR BOOK IS A CALL TO ACTION!

We define "elder" as anyone who has reached "normal retirement age," and our message is especially relevant for anyone on the threshold of retirement. The key is to follow our "Action Steps" and protect yourself before your mental capacity is diminished gradually by age or suddenly by a stroke or other disability. The time to plan is *now*.

We write for potential victims of financial abuse, but your children and your financial advisors should also read this book. They can help you through this potentially dangerous stage in your life.

Those who take advantage of the elderly do so because they think it will be easy. But if you make it difficult—simply by asking questions, or knowing when to end a conversation, or insisting on carefully reading any documents or sales materials, or arranging your finances so transparently that any financial abuse will be easily discovered—the bad guys, the con artists, will often simply move on.

IT'S NOT JUST ABOUT THE MONEY

Financial abuse means more than losing your retirement nest egg. It could mean losing your independence and being subject to fraud, coercion, intimidation, and isolation.

The risk of financial elder abuse is real. It has many dangerous aspects, and it should be alarming to all of us past retirement age. In *The MetLife Study of Elder Financial Abuse: Crimes of Occasion, Desperation, and Predation Against America's Elders*, a dire warning is issued for those who think elder financial abuse is only about the money:

> The findings from the research literature and cases reported in newsfeeds illustrate the dehumanization of victims that takes place in the process of financial abuse and creates an avenue to further victimization. Most obviously, and in almost all instances, the goals of financial exploitation are achieved through deceit, threats, and emotional manipulation of the elder. In addition to this psychological mistreatment, physical and sexual violence frequently occur within the vortex of elemental greed and disregard that surrounds financial abuse. Examples of physical attacks, neglect, rape and emotional abuse in the context of financial exploitation abound.... In some cases,

violence occurred during the perpetration of an isolated crime; in others, emotional control, threats, or neglect of care transpired over months and even years within close relationships....[2]

If that doesn't make you want to act, nothing will!

WHERE TO BEGIN

In the next few pages, we will explore why the elderly are targets, what makes the elderly vulnerable, and what we can do to respond and protect ourselves. We explain how to take *ten easy action steps* that will help you defend your financial assets and yourself against abuse. Here they are:

1. *We will define and help you understand elder financial abuse.* You can't protect yourself from abuse if you don't know what it is!
2. *We will teach you how to recognize potential abusers.* You can't protect yourself from potential abusers if you can't recognize them.
3. *We will help you admit that you're vulnerable.* It's nothing to be ashamed of, and overconfidence makes you more susceptible to abuse.

4. *We will teach you how to simplify your finances.* It's easier to protect your finances if you can keep track of them all!

5. *We will teach you how to make your finances transparent.* Transparency helps bring financial abuse to light.

6. *We will teach you how to organize your key financial, medical, and legal documents.* This makes it easier for you—and those who care for you—to execute tasks and spot abuse as soon as it happens.

7. *We will teach you how to protect your personal identity information (PII).* Unless you are totally "off the grid," you need to be extremely careful with information abusers want to exploit.

8. *We will help you create a circle of advisors.* Social isolation makes you more vulnerable to abuse.

9. *We will encourage you to consider naming a financial caregiver.* It need not be a paid position; you can choose a friend or relative.

10. *We will encourage you to work with a senior-friendly financial institution.* The more people in your corner, the better.

Is it possible to stop financial elder abuse? Yes! You'll learn how best to defend yourself against abuse with the ten easy action steps listed above.

Let us show you how.

ACTION STEP 1

RECOGNIZE THAT YOU ARE A TARGET

RECOGNIZE THAT YOU ARE A TARGET

The first step in stopping financial elder abuse is knowing the risks and recognizing that there are many different ways you can be targeted.

—

Here are just a few examples.

A son "borrows" $5,000 from his eighty-year-old mother, Miriam, who is suffering from Alzheimer's disease. He uses the money to buy drugs to feed his substance abuse habit. He has no intention of paying the money back, figuring that she will forget all about the loan in a few days. *Miriam is a victim of elder financial abuse.*

Mike, eighty years old, receives a call from someone claiming to be with the IRS. The "agent" tells Mike he will be arrested unless he pays his overdue taxes immediately. He is told to go to a local store and buy prepaid debit cards. Mike does so and reads the numbers on the back of the cards to the scammer. The scammer uses the numbers to steal the funds on the cards. *Mike is a victim of elder financial abuse.*

A caregiver convinces an elderly couple—the husband, Bob, has terminal cancer and the wife, Sandra, has Alzheimer's disease—that the care she provides is the only thing keeping them out of a nursing facility. She isolates the couple from friends and family. In the meantime, she slowly gains control over their assets. She starts spending their money and running up large balances on their credit cards. *Bob and Sandra are victims of elder financial abuse and emotional abuse.*

Lane, seventy-eight years old, has her purse in her shopping cart when another shopper purposefully distracts her while an accomplice snatches her wallet from the purse. Her wallet contains her driver's license and Medicare card (which plainly displays her Social Security number). Her Personally

Identifiable Information (PII) is sold to identity thieves on the internet and is used in several scams. *Lane is a victim of elder financial abuse and identity theft.*

Martha is eighty-seven years old. She receives a call from a perpetrator telling her she has won more than a million dollars and a new car in a foreign lottery. She is told that before receiving her winnings she will have to pay taxes and fees. Martha wires $5,000 to the caller over the next several days. The "winnings" are never paid and the car never shows up. *Martha is a victim of elder financial abuse.*

A daughter visits her mother, Dotty, for Christmas. Going through her mother's bank statements, she finds a check for $15,000 paid to a contractor several months earlier who insisted work on her home needed to be done to bring her septic tank "up to code." Dotty explains that the contractor was accompanied by a city official who confirmed the need for the repairs. The contractor took the money, but the work was never done. When Dotty tried to contact him, the phone just kept ringing. *Dotty is a victim of elder financial abuse.*

Jay is a seventy-five-year-old who considers himself a sophisticated investor. He believes the best return can be earned only from investments that are not regulated by the government. Over the years, he has responded repeatedly to phone calls from unregistered stock brokers offering him potentially "high reward" investments unregulated by the government. Despite terrible results (he has lost many thousands of dollars over the years), he continues to follow his investment "strategy." His name appears frequently on "mooch lists" bought and sold by investment fraudsters who know he is an easy target. *Jay is a victim of elder financial abuse and investment scams.*

Ralph is a seventy-six-year-old who has suffered from financial abuse and scams in the past, so he is overjoyed to receive a phone call from a firm that promises to recover his losses for a small fee. After he pays the fee, however, the firm disappears, and none of his original losses were recovered. *Ralph is a repeat victim of elder financial abuse.*

A doctor, who accepts Medicare, falsely diagnoses elderly patients with cancer and tells them surgery is needed. He performs unnecessary surgery on numerous patients, billing Medicare for the cost. *Each patient is a victim of elder financial abuse and the physical abuse of an unnecessary surgery.*

Sam attends an evening event for seniors at his local church. A speaker invites audience members to make an "ethical investment" of a thousand dollars each to help dig wells in needy African villages. But the spokesman is a fraudster, and the "ethical investment" is nothing more than a Ponzi scheme. *Sam and the other audience members are victims of elder financial abuse and "affinity fraud," in which the scammer infiltrates an organization (such as a church) and implements a scam that relies on members' preexisting mutual trust and familiarity.*

Do stories like these sound familiar? They should, because the truth is, elder financial abuse is an epidemic sweeping the country—and it makes us mad as hell, which is why we wrote this guide to avoiding it. Unless you're constantly on the lookout, you could be the next victim.

WHY ARE THE ELDERLY TARGETS FOR FINANCIAL ABUSE?

Many people assume senior citizens are targeted because they suffer from mental or physical decline.

The National Center on Elder Abuse, for instance, defines elder financial abuse as "the illegal taking, misuse, or concealment of funds, property, or assets of a vulnerable elder" at risk for harm by another due to changes in "physical functioning, mental functioning, or both."[1]

But the reality is, even if you are a physically and mentally healthy eighty-year-old, you are still a target for elder financial abuse. You are a target because of your age and your financial status, and because you are sitting on a retirement nest egg that someone wants to steal. Seniors are the most likely demographic to have savings, own their homes, and enjoy good to excellent credit scores, all of which make them targets—whether for financial abuse or identity theft. Criminals target the elderly because that's where the money is. A recent article in *Barron's* magazine pegged the wealth of those aged sixty-five and older at $18 trillion dollars! No wonder seniors are targets. In that same article, the author warned that the longer you live, the more likely you are to be relatively affluent; and by the age of eighty-five, seniors have nearly a 50% chance of suffering some degree of cognitive impairment.[2] People with bad intentions therefore see seniors as easy marks.

Other factors play into this as well. Social isolation is a big one; some senior citizens become so physically and emotionally dependent on their caregivers that they become their financial prisoners.

It's also true that many of us seniors slowly lose our ability to handle household finances or lose our spouse who handled them. David Laibson, a professor at Harvard University, argues that we reach our peak financial capability at fifty-three. It's all downhill from there! In desperation, too many seniors who don't want to burden family members seek financial help not from those best prepared to give it, but from scammers.

In the US Securities and Exchange Commission's report titled "Elder Financial Exploitation," released in June of 2018, the following factors are listed as ways of increasing the risk of elder financial exploitation:

- Physical and cognitive health issues
- A decline in financial capacity
- As we age, our ability to judge trustworthiness and financial riskiness declines
- Increasing social isolation
- The number of the vulnerable elderly is growing
- The elderly have money
- The nature of retirement assets has changed over the years—more elderly rely on a retirement nest egg (an IRA or 401(k) account) that can be targeted by criminals and less on pension payments that are more difficult to exploit[3]

Just as elderly persons become less and less able to protect themselves, so they become the target of financial exploitation. Sadly, elder financial abuse crimes often go unreported.

Elders fear that if they report a family member, they may be left abandoned and uncared for. A 2011 study titled "Under the Radar: New York State Elder Abuse Prevalence" concluded that only 2% of elder financial abuse incidents were reported.[4]

WHY *YOU* MIGHT BE A TARGET FOR FINANCIAL ABUSE

You are a target because *every* elderly person is a target. It doesn't matter where you live, how much money you have in the bank, or whether you are spry and happy or incapacitated and depressed. The abusers see every elderly person as someone they can take advantage of—they only have to vary their approach.

The sad fact is that even the characteristics that might make you a wonderful grandparent can make you an easy target. It is not just the isolated, naïve, or impaired elderly who are vulnerable; it is the open, friendly, and gregarious who might get a fraudulent midnight phone call saying, "Grandma, I'm in trouble and need bail money—and please don't tell mom and dad." It happens all the time.

Whatever your personality, whatever your financial, mental, emotional, or physical situation, scammers have you targeted. Action Step #1 is recognizing that you are a target for every aspect of financial elder abuse, from identity theft to fraudulent repairs, from sweepstakes scams to fake "Grandma, I'm in trouble" calls, from IRS impersonation scams to all the rest.

But as we'll see, you don't have to be a victim! Simple awareness of your vulnerability is the first step to avoiding that.

RECOGNIZE POTENTIAL ABUSERS

2

RECOGNIZE POTENTIAL ABUSERS

After forty years as a safety officer for a large corporation, Richard "Red" O'Keefe retired. He was a spry eighty-one-year-old, had never married, and lived alone frugally.

Red had no relatives with whom he was close, but his niece and nephew who lived nearby had recently gotten in touch. They encouraged him to retire and "take it easy." They also offered to help him manage his retirement portfolio of investments and benefits.

Before he retired, Red had to decide whether to roll his 401(k) account (which was worth about $300,000) into an IRA or purchase an annuity that would pay him about $3,000 a month for the rest of his life. Red's niece and nephew told him it was a mistake to lock his money into the annuity because he could always make withdrawals from an IRA, and at the same time, he could lend them money to "start a business," which would be an "investment." Red didn't know a lot about investing—and he wasn't much interested in learning—but he thought an annuity was a good fit for his needs, and he recognized that his niece and nephew did not have his best interests at heart—something that was proven when they stopped talking to him after he put his money in the annuity.

Red realized that retirement planning meant he had to think about his ability *today and in the future* to look after financial security and to fend off perpetrators of elder financial abuse. At age eighty-one, he was still in good physical and cognitive health, but he couldn't count on having the same degree of health five or ten years down the road. He knew he had to take steps to protect his financial security, and, for him, an annuity made sense.

Annuities aren't for everyone, but he knew that in his case, a steady stream of monthly income was less of a target for financial abusers than a large lump sum sitting in an IRA. The monthly annuity check would be deposited electronically into his checking account at the bank. His only other source of monthly income was his Social Security check, which was also deposited directly. He paid most of his bills online. He checked his account regularly.

Red recognized the threat of elder financial abuse, and shielded himself by employing the acronym STOP (which we will talk about in more detail later), making his finances Simple, Transparent, Organized, and Protected.

FAMILY AND FRIENDS CAN BE THE PERPETRATORS OF ELDER ABUSE

We told Red's story to make one big point. According to the National Adult Protective Services Association (NAPSA), most elder financial abuse is committed by the elderly person's *own family members*;[1] and, as a detailed study of elder financial abuse in Utah found, financial abuse by family members results in greater losses than financial abuse by strangers![2]

Red was not taken in by the professed interest of his niece and nephew in his financial well-being, but many people *are* taken in by family members who don't have their best interests at heart. Unfortunately, some family members just want to get their hands on the elderly parent's or relative's money. The financially abused elderly often excuse or justify the abuse because they believe their family is taking care of them, or they want to avoid arguments, or they rationalize that the money will go to family members eventually as part of their inheritance anyway, so what's wrong with giving them the money a little earlier? After all, they need the money now!

And it's not just family members, of course; it could be close friends of the family or even acquaintances and trusted personal friends. All are potential sources of elder financial abuse.

Some of these are "sweetheart" scams, the most familiar being an elderly gentleman falling in love with a much younger woman who is after his money. We are all vulnerable to a kind word or the promise of care and companionship as we get older—especially after losing a spouse—and it is all too easy to give such people unwarranted access to our bank accounts and power over our financial affairs.

Con artists who practice this game are very patient and very good at what they do. They start out slowly and their financial abuse grows over time. It starts with suggestions along the lines of: "Wouldn't it just be easier for you if my name was also on your checking account? I can help you make sure your bills are paid on time." Or they might say, "Why don't you invest me with your power of attorney? That way I can ensure that no matter what happens, you'll be looked after."

The National Adult Protective Services Association warns that the misuse of the power of attorney is very common.[3] Sometimes the power of attorney is obtained fraudulently from a person with dementia. Other times, the person granted power of attorney uses it to divert funds to himself or herself—funds that should be used for your care or left to your estate.

Sometimes, family, friends, acquaintances, and caregivers take actions that amount to outright theft, simply by stealing jewelry, money, or other valuables from an elderly person who might not immediately recognize their loss or be too intimidated to do anything about it. In one case, an adult daughter who had not visited her elderly mother in six months noticed some of her mom's favorite artwork was missing. Turns out, it was stolen by her mom's caregiver and sold off piece by piece.

Caregivers with bad intentions often attempt to keep the care recipient isolated. They are careful never to leave the side of the care recipient while others are visiting. They control the conversation and contact the care recipient has with the outside world to better hide the financial abuse.

One way to avoid caregiver financial abuse is to keep the *physical caregiving function* separate from the *financial caregiving function*. We will delve more into the financial caregiver function later.

TRUSTED ADVISORS CAN BE PERPETRATORS TOO

Even close professional advisors may take advantage of you because of your trust in them. This includes attorneys, financial planners, insurance sales professionals, doctors and other health care professionals, and even pastors.

How do you protect yourself from experts you assumed you could trust? Always ask questions; always ask for unbiased second opinions not only on health matters but on financial decisions; always research your options; and never let your guard down, even when you are talking with a licensed professional or someone with whom you share a political, religious, or social affinity. Those who commit elder financial abuse will take advantage of all these things to take advantage of *you*! They know the value of a title or a credential; they know that it provides them with power and authority. How many times have we heard stories about doctors committing Medicare fraud, or about self-dealing lawyers, or financial planners, or, regrettably, even religious leaders who take advantage of their own parishioners? No one is above suspicion. You don't need to be paranoid, but you do need to have independent, second opinions available to you, and to consider your options before making decisions.

NEVER TRUST STRANGERS

When we were young, many of us were told never to trust strangers. That advice is just as true now that we're old! If a stranger comes to your door to do repair work you didn't order, don't let him in. When you get an email from an address you don't recognize announcing that you've won a sweepstake you didn't enter, delete the email. When a notice suddenly appears on your computer screen—not from your own computer's antivirus system—saying that a virus has been found on your computer and that you need to call the number on the screen immediately for assistance, recognize that it's a scam: you will be asked for a credit card number to pay for a fix to a nonexistent problem.

Another frequent scam these days is the "IRS Impersonation Scheme." You receive a phone call from the Internal Revenue Service (IRS)—every taxpayer's worst nightmare. The IRS "agent" tells you that you owe back taxes along with interest and penalties. He or she threatens you with arrest by the local police department unless you come up with the money immediately. The agent tells you to withdraw $8,000 from your bank account and purchase gift cards with the money. You are instructed to call the agent back with the gift card numbers. And by the way, the agent says, don't discuss this with anybody. Intimidated, you head to the bank immediately. You withdraw $8,000 in cash. If you're lucky, the teller recognizes you and realizes this is an unusual transaction. The teller alerts her manager who stops you on the way out the door. He invites you into his office. Despite the warning you received not to discuss the matter with anyone else, you tell the manager what the money is for. He explains the basic nature of such scams and points out that:

- The IRS will never call a taxpayer to demand that payment be immediately delivered, nor will the agency call about taxes owed without first having mailed a letter to the taxpayer

- The IRS will never demand that a taxpayer pay taxes without giving you an opportunity to question or appeal the amount owed

- The IRS will never ask for a credit card, debit card, or gift card number over the phone, or require a taxpayer to use a specific payment method for taxes, such as a prepaid debit card or gift card

- The IRS will never threaten to send local police or other law enforcement to have a taxpayer arrested

You agree to let the manager contact the police and return the money to your account.

So, if you get a call from someone supposedly at the IRS, making outrageous threats of fining you or jailing you unless you immediately pay back taxes you didn't know you owed, recognize that it is just another scam. And be further warned: some of these scammers are quite sophisticated. They might know part of your social security number. They might even disguise their caller ID to make it look like they're calling from the IRS. But no real IRS employee will actually call you and threaten you like that. When in doubt, hang up and call the IRS directly to ask if there are any real problems with your taxes.

Scammers have a very carefully scripted approach to their victims. They appeal primarily to your emotions, not your reason. They use fear to create a sense of urgency and confusion. Their offers are typically unsolicited and made over the phone or, increasingly, via the Internet. During the conversation, the scammer will ask for a credit card number, a bank account number, or some other key personal information over the phone. Their goal could be anything from identity theft to predatory lending or reverse mortgage scams, Medicare fraud, investment/securities or insurance fraud, or a myriad of other scams.

All of us are vulnerable, and there is nothing to be ashamed of if you become a victim. What you must do is report it. Only by letting the authorities know can we hope to reduce or even end this silent epidemic.

ADMIT THAT YOU ARE VULNERABLE (WE ALL ARE)

ACTION STEP

3

ADMIT THAT YOU ARE VULNERABLE (WE ALL ARE)

onfident that you won't be the victim of elder financial abuse?

Think your experience and financial knowledge has grown over the years and that you're sharper now at age seventy than you were ten or twenty years ago?

Are you the sort who would say, "Let the perps try and take financial advantage of me and see how far they get! I accept the challenge."

According to the experts, your overconfidence means you are *more* vulnerable to elder financial abuse, not less! A joint study by DePaul University and the Rush University Medical Center found that "large declines in cognition and financial literacy have little effect on an elderly individual's confidence in their financial knowledge and essentially no effect on their confidence in managing their finances."[1] In other words, you might think you've gotten better with age when in fact, you've probably slipped a little. This makes you more vulnerable to bad actors who will play on your overconfidence.

Keep in mind, it does not take a disease like Alzheimer's to reduce your financial decision-making skills. Normal aging of the brain can result in older adults experiencing problems with household financial management. Unfortunately, the perps know this. The normal cognitive decline of the elderly is yet another reason why these criminals prey on us.

It is not a fair fight! The perps know the elderly are vulnerable but their elderly targets do not!

THE IMPACT OF OVERCONFIDENCE

Overconfidence not only makes you more vulnerable to elder financial abuse; it can also make the impact of that abuse worse, as a previously confident individual can become an emotional wreck. Feelings of humiliation can lead to depression. That's why it's essential to understand that elder financial abuse is common—no matter what your mental and physical circumstances—and not something for which you are personally at fault. You have been taken advantage of by a criminal.

But the fact that it is common does not mean we have to accept it. It means we need to take steps to stop it—or better yet, prevent it.

Your safety lies in taking precautions now so that you have a better chance of successfully handling your financial affairs in the future.

GOING ON THE OFFENSIVE

So let's even the playing field. Accept what the perps already know—that they are preying on you because *normal* brain-aging makes you more vulnerable, more forgetful, more easily confused, and less likely to recognize financial abuse when it happens. Even if you do figure it out, you are still less likely to report the crime. The sooner you accept that at least some mental decline is natural and inevitable, the sooner and more effectively you can protect yourself. Taking precautionary steps now will credit you later. Don't

wait for your family, friends, healthcare professionals or
social service workers to take the first steps. Now is the time
to do it yourself. No matter how large or small your nest
egg, it is valuable to you—and a target of financial predators.

STOP

The key to ensuring your financial security lies in the
acronym STOP.

We need to stop them. Remember this acronym. It is at
the heart of any intelligent strategy to protect your finances.
It means making your finances:

Simple

Transparent

Organized

Protected

The great thing about STOP is that you can implement
it at any age, at any time—including right now.

Let's go through the steps, starting with simplifying your
finances.

ACTION STEP 4

SIMPLIFY YOUR FINANCES

SIMPLIFY YOUR FINANCES

S implifying your finances begins with reviewing your finances, and for that, you should consult an expert or several, possibly including an attorney, an insurance professional, a tax return preparer, a financial planner, and an investment advisor.

Let's briefly review what some of these experts can bring to the table.

An *attorney* can ensure that you have all your legal documents properly prepared so that there are no legal questions about finances.

An *insurance professional* can do an analysis to help you determine if any of your old insurance policies still serve a purpose or should be cashed in or consolidated.

A *tax return preparer or advisor* can advise you on "taxable events" that might occur while you simplify your finances, perhaps while consolidating brokerage accounts. He can also help you limit your tax liabilities.

A *financial planner* can help you set your financial goals and show how to achieve them in the simplest way. He may also be your *investment advisor*. A good investment advisor can simplify your portfolio, make sure your investments are in line with your needs and goals, and create an *investment policy statement*. This statement will guide you and any other advisers you may have. It's a good way to keep investment scammers at bay.

It's ironic, but simplifying your finances starts with spending a little more time and money now so you can save a lot more time and money later. Don't let the need for professional assistance discourage you from taking action. It actually should encourage you to start putting your strategic team in place and simplifying your finances *now*!

Here are five reasons why simplifying your finances makes sense:

1. Your financial life will become more focused on *goals*, creating short-term and long-term financial strategies.

2. Simplifying your finances will simplify your income tax recordkeeping and tax return preparation—and who doesn't want that?

3. Your estate planning will be streamlined by making sure legal documents such as wills, trusts, and designated powers of attorney are up to date.

4. Simpler finances are easier to manage as you get older.

5. The simpler your finances are, the easier it will be for your financial consultants to advise and help you manage your assets.

So, now that you have your team in place and know the benefit of simplifying your finances, let's get started. How do you simplify? Here are the basics. It's an eight-step approach.

Step 1: Consolidate your checking accounts to the fewest number possible.

We understand that married couples often have separate accounts, but really, one should be enough, with

possibly a shared "petty cash" account. Also, set up your
checking account for *online access*. While you will want
to know your banker personally, online access offers
another layer of security when you use it to make
automatic deposits, which can be monitored and protected
by your bank.

PETTY CASH APPROACH

Back in the days before plastic, our businesses all had a
"petty cash" fund that allowed employees to purchase sup-
plies within a reasonable spending range. When the petty
cash was low, the holder of the fund would request that it
be replenished. The same approach can work well with your
caregiver or housekeeper.

Even though our "simplification" goal recommends having only one bank account, there is nonetheless good reason
to consider a second account for cases of shared access. If
you need to authorize a caregiver to make expenditures on
your behalf, our first choice is a credit card with relatively
low limits, though the ability to pay by check may sometimes be necessary. Access to a bank account should be
controlled by limiting the amount of cash that is in the
account. Don't put more cash in the account than is necessary to handle the required purchases. Add additional funds
as needed.

Step 2: Consolidate your savings accounts.

Set up the remaining account for *online access*.

Step 3: Consolidate your certificates of deposit and other time deposits.

Interest rates have been low over the past several years. Some readers will remember shopping for certificates of deposit at several local banks searching for the best interest rates. Lately, it has been a choice between earning an annual rate of .00000023% at your current bank versus earning .00000024% at the bank down the street. Okay, we're exaggerating a little. But you know what we mean if you've wandered from bank to bank fearing that one day they may charge you a negative rate of interest to deposit your money with them! This is bound to change. Consider consolidating your certificates of deposit at your local bank (another way of developing a personal relationship with your banker).

Step 4: Review your in-force life insurance and annuity policies.

We've worked with a lot of clients who have purchased policies and can't remember why they bought them or why they hang on to them. If that's the case, it might be time to cash them in. There may also be a deferred annuity contract or two you purchased years ago that you are not sure what to do with. It's time to do a thorough review of all the polices you own and determine which have value and which are no longer needed. In some cases, you may be able to consolidate the policies with no tax consequences by doing what's called a 1035 exchange. A new policy may better fit your changing financial goals. Work with an experienced, knowledgeable insurance professional. Some insurance professionals make their living off commissions while others work as consultants that charge an hourly fee. The key is finding someone knowledge whom you trust. That's not always easy, but it's worth shopping around to find the best fit for you.

MAKE SURE YOU'RE INSURED

When simplifying your checking and other accounts at a bank, pay attention to the FDIC deposit insurance limits and how the insurance works at FDIC insured banks. Go to https://www.fdic.gov/deposit/deposits/brochures/deposit-insurance-at-a-glance-english.html for information on what is covered and what is not.

Step 5: Consolidate your retirement nest egg.

When we write "consolidate" your retirement nest egg *we do not mean* consolidate your investments. We *do mean* the number of accounts you maintain. Keep your portfolio properly diversified among different asset classes in accordance with the sound investment guidance provided by your financial planner/investment advisor. The planner can make changes to consolidate your accounts while keeping your overall financial goals in mind.

Step 6: Go paperless.

By going paperless you avoid having your mailbox stuffed with all sorts of useful information for scammers. Do you have a mailbox with a flag on it to notify you when incoming mail has been delivered by the mail carrier, or that you have left outgoing mail for the carrier to pick up? That little red flag is an invitation to scammers that something worth grabbing may be in your mailbox! By going paperless, those credit card statements, utility bills, and bank statements are no longer left in your mailbox. Even if your mailbox is secured, going paperless allows you to shred and throw out those accumulated statements that leave a nice paper trail for anyone gaining entrance to your home. While it's true that going paperless is not without its disadvantages—especially keeping your online information protected—the benefits outweigh the risks.

Step 7: Make use of electronic payments and deposits.

An important part of going paperless is making sure most deposits to your account and most payments you make are electronic. Yes, we know this is an adjustment for many of you, and we know that some of you out there have never even owned a computer. Owning a computer and managing your household finances online will be one of the most important steps you can take to simplify your finances and help protect you from financial abuse. It puts you in charge of your household finances in ways you never thought possible.

SELECTIVE USE OF AUTOMATIC PAYMENTS

Like most conveniences, automatic payments have a downside. When you don't receive a statement each month, you become less aware of your spending and you are more likely to spend beyond your means. We suggest that you limit automatic recurring payments to payments that are essential, things like your mortgage and insurance—payments that would cause great harm if missed.

Step 8: Review all your assets.

As we get older, we find we've accumulated a lot of valuable stuff, including home decorations, jewelry, and other expensive items that make nice targets not just for burglars but for con artists who will try to talk their way into your home to walk out of it with your valuables. So be careful and inventory your assets. Make the inventory available to others who can help you keep an eye on things.

FOR SNOWBIRDS

Many retirees spend their winters in a warmer part of the country, which means they might have two seasonally "local" banks, but the same principle applies: become a familiar banking client at both locations.

SIMPLIFYING IS SIMPLE

Simplifying your finances is really all a matter of common sense financial management to ensure your income and your assets align properly with your financial plan. A well designed and implemented plan will make you less vulnerable to financial scams. If you don't want to use (or can't afford) a financial planner, your local banker can help you. While it is important to consult the professionals—whether they be financial planners or bankers—the first step is your own commitment to clean your financial attic so that you (and trusted others) can better manage and keep track of your finances. So why delay? The time to start simplifying your life, protecting your assets, and committing to a long-term financial strategy is now.

THE IMPORTANCE OF GOOD BANKING RELATIONSHIPS

In this age of internet banking, there is one key relationship that is often overlooked—the relationship between you and your local bank or credit union. If you don't already have a good relationship with a local bank or credit union, you should establish one. Visit the branch every month and get to know the tellers and the branch manager. We suggest consolidating your banking activities because it is to your advantage if the bank's long-term employees know you. Nowadays, financial institutions train their employees to recognize a customer who has cognitive issues and is struggling to understand a transaction or may be the victim of financial elder abuse. So if pulling a team of professionals together is beyond your means, at least make sure you develop a good, long-term relationship with the local branch of a bank or credit union. Visit the branch regularly as you take care of your financial transactions and get know the people. They may even have hot coffee and cookies for you in the lounge area!

RESOURCES

There are plenty of books on simplifying and organizing your finances. These resources go well beyond what we can review here. From the surprise bestseller *The Life-Changing Magic of Tidying Up: The Japanese Art of Decluttering & Organizing* by Marie Kondo to *Get It Together: Organize Your Records So Your Family Won't Have To* by Melanie Cullen, there are many books that give you good places to start. A good book aimed at family caregivers is a *Checklist for Family Caregivers: A Guide to Making It Manageable* by Sally Balch Hurme (published in 2015 by the American Bar Association and AARP).

MAKE YOUR FINANCES TRANSPARENT

MAKE YOUR FINANCES TRANSPARENT

e've gone over why the S in our STOP strategy stands for *simplify*. Now, we'll go over why the T stands for *transparency*.

What does transparency really mean? It means shining a bright light on your simplified income and expenses, so that it is easy—*transparent*—to see what money comes in, what money goes out, and how your financial income and outflow fits into your overall strategic financial plan. Those who would take advantage of you would rather operate in the shadows, where what they do can't be seen by you or you those who would protect you.

One of the main risk factors for elder financial abuse is isolation. Scammers know that if an elderly person is isolated or can be intimidated into silence, then they are vulnerable. But if your finances are transparent, if you have a local banker who is well aware of your financial plan, you have an extra layer of protection.

As we know, scammers can come from any background. Some of them can even pose as caregivers. At first, the scammer will make it appear they are doing you a favor. They want to help you manage your finances. They want to protect you, watch out for you, and make life easier for you. Eventually, they will suggest you provide them with access to a few of your accounts.

If an individual tries to isolate you, then that's a warning sign they don't have your best interests at heart. A scammer might try to isolate you slowly at first. He'll start taking over your trips to the bank. He'll always be at your side when family members come to visit. He will warn you not to disclose your financial information to anyone besides him, because after all, everyone else is only interested in getting their hands on your money. In the end, the scammer may even use intimidation to keep you quiet.

Vampires cannot stand the light of day. Neither can financial scammers stand the light of transparency on their activities. You want to make your financial information transparent to a small circle of trusted family members, friends, and professional advisors who can provide such light.

For example, you can provide online access to your accounts to family members and trusted friends. Such access can be "read only," meaning it does not include the ability to conduct transactions within the account. Alternatively, you can have copies of your account statements sent directly to someone you trust.

Let everyone you deal with know that someone is always watching over your shoulder!

REMEMBER YOUR FRIENDLY NEIGHBORHOOD BANKER

We've mentioned this before, but it bears repeating: if you don't already have a good relationship with a local financial institution, establish one. Your friendly neighborhood banker is like a cop on the beat in your financial neighborhood. He can help you watch out for scammers.

The Consumer Financial Protection Bureau (CFPB) of the federal government recognizes that financial institutions can play a key role in reducing elder financial abuse. In March 2016, the CFPB released its "Recommendations and report for financial institutions on preventing and responding to elder financial exploitations." It noted that:

Some indicators of elder fraud risk may not match conventionally accepted patterns of suspicious activity, but nevertheless may be unusual in light of a particular account holder's regular pattern of behavior. Financial institutions can ensure that their systems consider the type of account-related activity that may be associated with elder fraud risk. The following is a sample of the types of account activity that may be associated with elder financial exploitation:

Atypical ATM card use

Uncharacteristic non-sufficient funds activity or overdraft fees

Activity in previously inactive accounts

Change of address on account

Opening new joint checking account or adding joint owner to existing account

Increase in total monthly cash withdrawals compared to historical pattern

Automated Clearing House (ACH) payment to a recipient with no history of ACH transactions with the customer

Missing recurring deposits

Electronic bill payments to new vendors

Atypical use of wire transfers

Unusual gaps in check numbers[1]

If you have a strong relationship with the tellers and branch manager of your local bank, they will be far more likely to notice these sorts of changes in your banking habits and thereby help guard you from financial abuse.

In addition, many financial institutions are now training their employees to be especially helpful to elderly customers whose cognitive abilities might be failing and who are therefore more vulnerable to financial abuse. The CFPB sees employee training as critical in the effort to prevent, detect and respond to elder financial exploitation. Clear, efficient training protocols enhance financial institutions' capacity to detect financial exploitation of elder customers. It is essential that training programs prescribe a protocol for actions to take when employees detect problems. Training should communicate the roles and responsibilities of management, frontline staff, and other employees to reduce ambiguity and promote efficient and timely action when staff suspect or observe elder financial exploitation.[2]

Remember: the banker and tellers at your local financial institution are there to help you safeguard your savings and protect you from financial abuse. Take full advantage of their professional assistance! They want to help.

THE VALUE OF TRANSPARENCY

Financial transparency is important, but the idea is not always easy to accept. Many of us naturally believe that our finances should be kept private, that they are "no one else's business," and that it is wrong to talk about them. We might think this is particularly true with our grown children, because talking about money can be complicated with questions about wills, power of attorney, and other issues.

But aging brings about physical and cognitive changes that we cannot ignore. Aging also makes us increasingly vulnerable to financial abuse that can cause long term psychological, physical, and emotional damage. The damage can wreck the remaining years of our lives. That's why it's important to take precautions, and simplifying your finances to make them more transparent is a necessary first step.

Here's how to get started: make your finances more transparent by allowing family members and trusted friends to gain access to your financial information. Provide them with "read only" access to your online accounts. Have copies of account statements mailed if you are not yet online.

Create a small circle of advisors that may include your accountant and attorney, family members, healthcare professionals, insurance professionals, adult children, and trusted friends whose opinion you value. It can be formal or informal. Encourage them to talk to each other and, if possible, meet periodically.

Can't afford that small circle of advisors? Get to know your local banker or manager of the nearby credit union. (You should anyway.)

Never allow yourself to become socially isolated! If you are homebound, use the phone. Ask people to visit. Become suspicious if a caregiver tries to keep you isolated from your friends and family.

Have "the conversation" with your adult children and trusted friends about your finances and how you want to protect yourself from financial abuse. It might seem awkward at first, but you'll likely be surprised at how understanding they will be, and how willing to help.

ADULT PROTECTIVE SERVICES (APS)

If you believe someone is trying to financially exploit you, take action. Don't hesitate to call the police if that person is present and represents an immediate danger. Is a home repair man trying to bully you into paying for work he has yet to complete? Is he standing on your front porch making you feel that you are in physical danger? If you can do so safely, call the police. But never put yourself in immediate danger. Give in to his demands until you can get yourself out of danger. In emergencies, call 911.

For financial and other types of abuse in which there is no immediate danger, call the local office of Adult Protective Services, or APS. For more information, go to www.napsa-now.org.

ORGANIZE YOUR KEY FINANCIAL, MEDICAL, AND LEGAL DOCUMENTS

ACTION STEP

6

ORGANIZE YOUR KEY FINANCIAL, MEDICAL, AND LEGAL DOCUMENTS

Organizing your financial, medical, and legal records—
which is very much like simplifying your finances and
making them more transparent—is an important way
to protect yourself as you get older. You need to do this *now*,
because the longer you wait, the more difficult it's likely to
be, as your cognitive skills slowly decline and your ability to
manage your own finances becomes more impaired. You
want to get your affairs in order *before* this happens. And
remember, you might not even be aware that your capacity
for handling your finances is diminishing. Here are six

warning signs—identified by scholars Kristen L. Triebel and Daniel C. Marson in their article "The Warning Signs of Diminished Financial Capacity in Older Adults," published by the Generations Journal of the American Society on Aging—that indicate you might not have the financial skills you once did:

1. *Memory lapses* resulting in errors, including failing to pay bills on time or missing payments altogether.
2. *Disorganization* that leads to losing important documents and missing important deadlines (especially tax return deadlines!).
3. *Declines in checkbook management skills.*
4. *Arithmetic mistakes*, including everything from making change, to computing a tip, to balancing your checkbook.
5. *Conceptual confusion* regarding such basic financial matters as mortgages, insurance products, and your will.
6. *Impaired judgment* that might manifest itself in a sudden interest in get-rich-quick schemes or unnecessary financial anxiety.[1]

Our STOP strategy—making your finances simplified, transparent, organized, and protected—is designed to address each of these warning signs, even if your financial skills were never that great to begin with. Getting your important papers together and in order is a big part of that, so you can better care for yourself while you can and so your trusted caregivers can take over when you can't.

GETTING STARTED—AND GETTING ORGANIZED

There are entire books dedicated to showing you how to organize your important documents. One we can recommend is *Get It Together: Organize Your Records So Your Family Won't Have To*, by Melanie Cullen with Shae Irving, J.D.

But here are some simple pointers.

Make a list of your most important legal, financial, and medical documents.

Once you have the list, put those documents in clearly marked, easily accessed files.

Make sure your will is up to date, with your property (house, car, items of sentimental value) and financial effects (not just cash, but savings plans, insurance policies, and government benefits) accounted for and assigned as you want them.

Leave detailed instructions for everything that might need to be done in the event of your incapacity or death—including the gamut from how to clean and care for your pets, to club memberships that might need to be canceled, to funeral arrangements.

Remember, too, that while we're organizing, we're simplifying—and that means shredding every unnecessary, unneeded, out-of-date paper. We want clean, comprehensive, and concise files that make it easy for you to find the information you need and easy for trusted family members and advisors to help you. Dusty stacks of waste paper, on the other hand, need to go into the waste paper basket. And don't just toss old papers—shred them so there's no paper trail that can be used by identity theft scammers.

Of course, many of your important documents, files, and memberships are likely online. We'll talk more about this in the next chapter, but you might want to take advantage of password management programs that allow you to document and store your usernames, passwords, and codes. If you do use such programs, you will also want to leave clear instructions so that trusted family members or advisors can access these programs when you no longer can.

YOUR HEALTH RECORDS

Keeping track of your medical records is a subject in itself. *My Body Passport* by Wendy and Laura Coulson, PhD, and *My Personal Health Record Keeper* by the Peter Pauper Press are two excellent resources.

The bottom line, though, is that you need to get your medical records in order—not just so you can refer to them, but also in case you become incapacitated and need someone else to make decisions on your behalf.

Your medical and financial interests are, of course, intertwined. Your family or trusted friends will need to track your physician care to protect your medical interests and track your healthcare expenses to protect your financial interests. They will also need to watch out for signs of identity theft and Medicare fraud (which can happen if a scammer steals your Medicare claim number).

You'll want organized health records to keep track of:

- Your medications (prescription and over the counter), frequency of use (daily or "as needed"), and dosage
- Where your medications are purchased (at a local pharmacy or mail order)
- Vitamins and supplements

- Vaccination records
- Contact information for doctors, dentists, and optometrists
- Your personal and family health histories
- Emergency room visits and hospital stays
- Your health insurance
- Recent blood test results

Generally, your financial and medical information is safer online than in your mailbox, but it is important to periodically print and retain a paper copy of your bank statements or medical records as a backup, in case your online accounts are hacked. In the next chapter, we'll look at strategies for protecting your online information.

ACTION STEP 7

PROTECT YOUR PERSONAL IDENTITY INFORMATION (PII)

PROTECT YOUR PERSONAL IDENTITY INFORMATION (PII)

We've come to the P in our STOP acronym. Making your finances Simple, Transparent, and Organized is your offensive game plan, but you need to play defense, too. That's where Protection comes in. In an increasingly online world, you need to protect your Personal Identity Information (PII) from online predators.

Your Personal Identity Information is any data that could potentially identify you. It includes your Social Security number, Medicare claim number, driver's license number, savings and checking account numbers, and passport information. For the online predator, every bit of information is valuable. On the "dark web," PII is bought and sold every day. The "dark web" refers specifically to websites that exist on an encrypted network and cannot be found by using traditional search engines (such as Google or Bing) or visited by using traditional browsers.

MEDICARE CLAIM CARDS

It is hoped that the new Medicare claim cards—issued in 2018 and 2019—will help reduce Medicare fraud, which costs taxpayers billions of dollars each year. As usual, however, whenever a change takes place, scammers will try and take advantage of it. Defend yourself by remembering that Medicare cards are free. If anyone contacts you asking you to "buy" a new card, it's a scam; if anyone calls you asking for your personal information so they can send you a card, that too is a scam.

The new Medicare cards will be mailed to every person who is on Medicare. They will have new account numbers to better protect your identity (it will no longer be a Social Security number). Your Medicare benefits will not change. One thing you may want to do is make sure the Social Security Administration (which administers Medicare) has your current address. Go to www.socialsecurity.gov or www.medicare.gov and confirm your contact information.

You need to protect your PII because online thieves can use the information to commit identity theft.

According to the Federal Trade Commission (the FTC) identity theft occurs "if someone is using your personal or financial information to make purchases, get benefits, file taxes, or commit fraud."[1] Nowadays we think of identity theft as something that occurs primarily online. While that is true, identity theft can also take place when someone steals your wallet and obtains your driver's license and your Medicare card. It can also occur when a thief goes through your garbage for bank or credit card statements. Some thieves may even look in your mailbox for incoming or outgoing mail that contains valuable PII.

Now, this all may seem scary, but by following a few commonsense tips, you can dramatically reduce the chances of your being a victim of identity theft.

Precautions as simple as these can make a big difference:

- Shred old documents you no longer need
- Keep your tax returns and other sensitive documents in a locked file
- Use a post office box rather than an unsecured mailbox
- Lock your doors and windows—even when you're home

- Keep track of who has a key to your home

THE PROBLEM

Here's a number that staggered us—in 2014, the US Department of Justice estimated that 17.6 million Americans were identity theft victims. The FTC handles more than 500,000 complaints a year related to identity theft. The predators are persistent, creative, and ruthless in their attempts to breach your online security and seize your personal information.

If they succeed, they might:

- Open credit cards in your name (you'll find out when you receive the first credit card statement in the mail)
- Apply for federal and state tax refunds in your name (when you file your actual return, you'll discover that someone has already collected your refund)
- Take out a loan in your name (you'll get a call from a collection agency when the new loan goes unpaid)

- Obtain medical care using your Medicare claim card

Because of these crimes you may be:

- Denied credit/loans
- Denied medical care
- Harassed by debt collectors
- Subject to a lawsuit

Additionally, undoing the damage caused by identity theft may take many hours of your time and add stress, anxiety, and even embarrassment to your life.

KNOW WHAT'S ON YOUR CREDIT REPORT

It's important to get a copy of your credit report and make sure that the information is accurate. But don't pay for a credit report—you are entitled to a free report each year from each of the three major credit reporting agencies. Be cautious with online services that seem to offer credit-related services. There is only one online site that provides your credit report without a fee: www. AnnualCreditReport.com.

If you are ever a victim of identity theft, you should go immediately to www.identitytheft.gov. This site is run by the Federal Trade Commission (FTC) and will help you report the identity theft and create a recovery plan.

But wouldn't you rather avoid identity theft altogether than deal with its aftermath? What follows are some simple steps that will reduce, though not eliminate, the chance that you will be a victim of online identity theft.

SOME SIMPLE GUIDELINES TO FOLLOW

The following are common sense tips to reduce your chance of being an identity theft victim.

Password tips

Never share your passwords or PIN (personal identification number) with anyone. But there's one exception: when an individual dies, his passwords, PINS, and online accounts die with him. This is an increasing problem; no one has access to the information necessary to set that individual's affairs in order. When you do your estate planning, your attorney should advise you on storing your online information in a place available to your family or executor in case of an emergency.

Use a complicated password based on an easy-to-remember phrase rather than a simple, one-word password containing a few numbers. For example, the phrase "Rick graduated from high school in 1970!" would be RGHSin1970! Use your imagination—don't make it easy for the predators.

Is the website legitimate?

Online predators sometimes set up phony websites that include the name or logo of a well-known bank or retailer hoping to attract Internet users. To make sure you are going to a legitimate site, use a search engine such as Google or Bing. For example, if you do a Google search for Chase Bank the very first site listed will likely be a legitimate site. Based on a Google search, this is what we got:

https://www.chase.com/

That address is known as the URL (for uniform resource locator). When being referred to a site of a familiar organization, be alert to the spelling used in the URL and the way that the URL is structured—scammers will often take possession of a slightly misspelled version, or use the correct spelling in a section of a more complex URL. Be alert!

Some websites now use "2 factor authentication" (2FA), meaning that once you input your username and password, you will be sent a verification code via email. You will not be allowed into the site until you enter the verification code. This added level of security can be very reassuring.

If the URL starts with https:// that means it is secure (that's what the "s" in the https stands for). This means no one can read your username and password except your browser and the website.

And by the way, did you ever notice that to the left of the URL is a tiny padlock? If it is green and shut, that means the site is certified as being owned by the organization it represents. Note that www.chase.com has a tiny, locked green padlock to the left of its URL. If the padlock is red and open, the site is not certified. If that is the case, you may not want to enter your login details. Best to leave the site.

Email attachments and links

Be suspicious if any email is marked "urgent" and/or "confidential."

Be very careful when it comes to opening attachments. Don't open email attachments from anyone you don't recognize or have not had contact with before. Even a familiar name on the email can be misleading. Scammers are getting better at sending out emails with familiar names and logos, such as the logo of your bank. Someone the authors know (who knows better) told us he came very close to responding to an email that appeared to come from his bank. The name and logo looked legitimate. The message that someone had used his debit card to make a large purchase for $341.43 at a store he frequented also appeared realistic (he immediately thought someone had bought a large screen TV at his expense). How would the scammer know he shopped at the store often? Panicky, he was tempted to respond to the email immediately. He stopped himself, however, and called the customer service number on the back of his card. Sure enough, the email was a scam. The company that issued his debit card confirmed that there was no such purchase on his card from that store. He was warned not to respond to the email but to forward it to their fraud detection unit. He was also told to delete the email as soon as he forwarded it (which he did). An hour later, the fraud detection department sent him an email confirming the first email was indeed a scam.

The lesson? Slow down! Review your emails carefully and always keep your guard up!

Don't click on a link that appears in a junk email. As a rule, don't click on any link from anyone or any company or organization you don't recognize or have not had contact with before. It is extremely unlikely you won the Australian lottery, or any other foreign lottery, for that matter. Ignore the email. Don't open it! Delete it.

If an email makes a promise that is too good to be true, it probably isn't true. Delete it.

Social network

Social networks can be fun and keep you in touch with the important people in your life. Just make sure you don't disclose too much information on your social network site. Don't give away your vacation plans and the dates of your trip! By reading your social media site, thieves will know exactly when you will be gone and when no one will be home! Pictures of you at the airport holding up your passport provides predators with a feast of information.

Antivirus and firewall protection

Use antivirus protection and firewall software on your computer.

"FREEZING" YOUR CREDIT

At eighty-three, Paul was a long-time participant in Medicare, but this was the first time anyone from "Medicare" had ever called him. The caller asked Paul for his Medicare claim number. At first suspicious, Paul relaxed when the representative provided the first three digits of his number and told Paul to give him the remaining digits and the letter following the number. That way, the representative said, "We can both be sure that we are talking to the right person." Paul gave the caller the rest of his identification number and proceeded to answer all the caller's other questions, including questions about his credit cards. When Paul told his son the story, his son called the Medicare fraud line at 800-447-8477 and initiated a "credit freeze."

A credit freeze prevents anyone from opening a new account in your name. The three major credit reporting agencies—Equifax, TransUnion, and Experian—can put a block on the use of your credit information. Freezing your credit will have no impact on your current loans or credit cards, but it will protect you from a scammer opening new accounts in your name. To establish new accounts, he will have to "thaw" your credit using a personal identification number (PIN) that only you know. You can freeze your credit online by going to each agency's website, or by submitting a request via certified mail.

To adequately protect your credit, you will need to do this with each of the three agencies. There is a small fee to freeze and another fee to thaw your credit, but in many states, there is a senior discount. Most of the states allow for a permanent freeze, but residents of Kentucky, Nebraska, Pennsylvania, and South Dakota will have to repeat the process every seven years.

Credit monitoring is another layer of protection that will alert you when an inquiry is made about your credit. For a free monitoring service, visit www.CreditKarma.com.

Other

Do not use public computers or open networks at restaurants, coffee shops, retail outlets, libraries, or anywhere else, to access sensitive information. "Trust but verify" is a translation from an old Russian proverb, made famous by Ronald Reagan. Type it in large, bold print. Tape it somewhere on your computer or laptop!

PASSWORD MANAGEMENT PROGRAMS

Because hackers are so active, many online accounts require you to change your password on a regular basis. For most of

KEEPING ADEQUATE BACKUPS

These days, most of us store our financial records electronically. Bank statements, tax returns, loan and lease documents, and any number of other documents are easily scanned and saved on a computer. But hackers are lurking. They're not just after your credit file; they will also threaten to lock down your computer and hold your data hostage. Having paper backup files or USB memory sticks that have your up-to-date files is an absolute necessity. If you are not sure how to make backup files, ask your son or daughter or hire an IT consultant for a couple of hours (IT consultants are plentiful and not expensive). Once you have a backup routine, you'll enjoy the confidence of knowing that your data is secure.

us, it's nearly impossible to remember all the passwords to our financial accounts. There has to be a written list, but that list could be stolen. How do we solve that problem? With a password management program that retains all your passwords in a secure database, and that you access with a single "master" password. Before you buy a password management program, make sure that it uses "two-step authentication." That sounds complicated, but it's really just an extra layer of security—requiring a second verification code after your password.

Some of the programs also have protocols for releasing your master password to authorized persons if you are incapacitated or dead, but you might feel more comfortable leaving your access code information in a sealed envelope with your attorney or with a trusted friend or family member.

CLOSE YOUR BROWSER WHEN YOU'RE DONE

When using your computer to access your financial accounts—bank accounts, brokerage accounts, credit card accounts, or any other account that has sensitive information—always log out and then close your browser window. Don't make it easy for someone to sit down and access your account.

A FINAL WORD

The website www.grandpad.net offers computer tablets that come pre-loaded with senior-friendly software and added security to protect you from online identity theft. They aren't for everybody, and they come with some drawbacks, such as a limited ability to browse the web.

Other good online resources for protecting yourself can be found at https://staysafeonline.org and http://www.connectsafely.org.

In addition, local community colleges often offer classes on computers and computer security for seniors.

CREATE A CIRCLE OF ADVISORS

CREATE A CIRCLE
OF ADVISORS

We want to add another element to your offensive game plan. As you get older, you need to work hard to keep from becoming socially isolated. Your health and finances will benefit if you stay socially engaged. In this chapter, we show you how to do that by creating a circle of advisors.

Your circle can be a formal, paid group of advisors consisting of your attorney, your accountant, and a healthcare professional. Or it could be an informal circle of family members,

friends, and neighbors. You can meet with them regularly or
merely chat with them on the phone. The important thing is
not that they are experts, though having expertise is fine; it
is that you trust their judgment, respect their opinions, and
feel comfortable asking them questions.

That doesn't mean that they necessarily know more than
you do, or that you are in any way obligated to follow their
advice, but it never hurts to have a few friends you can turn
to when you have to make an important decision. Consulting
with your circle of advisers might help you avoid big mistakes.

—

Alice was approached by an insurance salesman offering final expense insurance. At her death, $10,000 would
be paid to cover her burial expenses. There was just one
thing: the details of the plan were available only after she
paid the first month's premium. It was state law, he
explained. She would have thirty days after paying the
premium to review the material. If she decided to cancel
the policy, she could go ahead and do so. She would receive
a refund of her premium. Otherwise, she could keep the
policy. Alice called her friend Miriam to discuss the offer.
Miriam had worked in the insurance industry, and told

Alice this was a scam. *Nothing in state law prohibits you from reviewing a policy before you buy it*, she said. State law *does* protect you by giving you a thirty-day period to change your mind and get your money back—but that won't help if you're dealing with a scam artist who will soon disappear with your money.

Alice was embarrassed that she almost fell for the scam, but she should have taken pride in seeking guidance from a well-informed friend. Circles of advisors, formal and informal, succeed because they share knowledge and experience that help you make considered decisions.

IMPORTANCE OF SOCIAL CONNECTIONS

Social engagement—having healthy, supportive relationships with friends and family—is linked to wellbeing as you age. Social engagement enables higher cognitive functioning, while reducing the likelihood of Alzheimer's disease and other dementias. In contrast, social isolation is linked to poor health and depression. It is a prime culprit in making the elderly vulnerable to financial abuse.

We know that staying socially engaged is not easy. Old friends may have moved away or died. If you have "aged in place" you might find, as many seniors do, that your neighborhood has changed dramatically, and you no longer feel connected to your neighbors. Your grown children might live in a different state and rarely have time to visit you. Poor physical or cognitive health might limit your ability to entertain friends or attend social functions or go to your place of worship.

But even though it's not easy, making the effort to stay socially engaged, as far as you are able, will pay you physical, mental, and emotional rewards, as well as build your informal circle of advisers.

A "PROFESSIONAL" CIRCLE OF ADVISORS?

Sometimes you might want a professional circle of advisors to help with complex legal, financial, and long-term medical issues. In our experience, these key players in an elderly person's life—doctors, lawyers, financial planners—seldom, if ever, talk to one another. If you can bring them together for a meeting or a conference call once or twice a year, it will be well worth whatever hourly fee they charge you. This professional circle of advisers can help ensure that your STOP plan of Secure, Transparent, Organized, and Protected finances is working.

If you don't have a team of professional advisers, ask your friends and family for recommendations, and consult professional organizations like the Aging Life Care Association (www.aginglifecare.org) to find qualified care managers and The National Academy of Elder Law Attorneys (www.naela.org) to find lawyers who specialize in elderly issues.

If hourly fees are beyond your budget, then consider securing legal help through a legal insurance plan that can be purchased for a modest monthly fee. Such lawyers might not be able to attend adviser meetings, but they can prepare the wills, trusts, and other documents you might need.

YOUR VIRTUAL CIRCLE OF ADVISORS

Technology can help you stay socially connected. While a computer connection is no replacement for direct human contact, it can be of great assistance if you or your friends are largely homebound.

Many experts refer to the "digital divide" that separates older seniors (those over seventy-five) and baby boomer seniors (those over sixty-five). Older seniors are less likely to be familiar with technology that now encompasses laptop computers, smart phones, desktop computers, and tablets. But that divide is shrinking because seniors are finding large screen tablets easy to use, especially ones like the GrandPad offered at https://www.grandpad.net. It is a tablet with its own private, secure connectivity system (via Verizon) and built-in technical support to get you started. You cannot "surf the Internet" on the GrandPad tablet, but you also won't be inundated with junk emails full of scams. What you can do is set up your own private family network and your virtual circle of advisors. In addition to sending emails, you can make calls and send and receive photos. You can also share videos and make video calls.

Oscar Senior (https://www.oscarsenior.com) is another useful tool. It can be downloaded through the App Store and Google Play Store to your tablet to increase its security and ease of use.

If you are "computerphobic," we urge you to be brave and reconsider your aversion to technology. Going online with some of these secure, user-friendly products can reconnect you with friends and family, and help you better protect your health and financial security.

CONSIDER NAMING A FINANCIAL CAREGIVER

CONSIDER NAMING A FINANCIAL CAREGIVER

PREPARING FOR THE UNEXPECTED

There will come a day when we're unable to carry on business as usual. That day might arrive suddenly or more likely, we'll get there gradually. So what should we do to prepare? For starters:

- Have a written plan that outlines what should be done if you become physically or mentally incapable of conducting your financial affairs

- Inform family members about your plan
- Prepare a healthcare power of attorney, and let that person know how you want your care conducted
- Set up direct deposits for your Social Security and other recurring income
- Implement automatic payments of your important, recurring bills
- Review your insurance policies with an agent to confirm that you are properly covered
- Select a "financial caregiver"—someone who can keep your finances in good working order

If you are elderly and single, the argument for appointing a financial caregiver is easy to make. That person is there to make sure your finances are looked after—both now and later, when you are unable to look after them yourself.

But what if you are married? Is a financial caregiver needed? Yes! Let's first consider a scenario that is all too common, when one spouse is taking care of a chronically or terminally ill partner and, contrary to expectations, the caregiver spouse passes away suddenly. Is there someone who can step in and manage the surviving spouse's finances? If you have a financial caregiver appointed—and you've followed our STOP program with a simplified, transparent, organized, and pro-tected accounting of your assets—the caregiver can step in and take over with minimum fuss during a difficult time.

Ideally, you want to appoint your financial caregiver early in your senior days. The caregiver can be an adult son, daughter or trusted friend. But the sooner you establish a long-term relationship with a financial caregiver, the better they will understand your finances and your needs. So don't delay!

CHECKS AND BALANCES

No matter how much you trust your financial caregiver, it is important that your finances remain true to our STOP strategy of secure, transparent, organized, and protected. It is prudent to apply some checks and balances to the caregiver's authority. For example, give online "read only" access to your bank accounts to more than one individual, or send paper statement copies to another trusted individual who can act as your backup financial caregiver. If you allow your financial caregiver to pay your bills, make sure he does so from a separate account with limited funds. Instruct your bank to transfer sufficient funds for short-term needs every month or two weeks. Restrict access to your larger accounts, which should be set aside for long-term investing. You should not share an account with anyone but your spouse, because no one should have unlimited access to your money.

GETTING DOWN TO BASICS

A financial caregiver helps you manage your money and other assets so that you don't have to worry about them. It is important to note that this is an *evolving relationship*. As you need more assistance, the financial caregiver does more for you, but *you* control the relationship, giving the financial caregiver more responsibility only when you are ready.

Most financial caregiving relationships are *informal* and not based on a legal authorization, such as a power of attorney. This means the financial caregiver cannot make decisions without your approval and will not be able to sign checks or sell your assets. The downside to having an informal relationship is that the financial caregiver has no real authority and has no fiduciary obligation to act in your best interest. In addition, there is no legal record of the relationship.

It is a *collaborative* position—the financial caregiver works alongside you.

A financial caregiver is not paid for his or her assistance. A financial caregiver is not a financial professional, but is a trusted family member or friend.

WHY RELY ON A FINANCIAL CAREGIVER?

Early in your relationship, your financial caregiver might be more of an informal financial advisor, rather than an executor of any duties. Later, a financial caregiver may help with day-to-day finances and help you plan for future financial needs. As your ability to handle your finances decreases, the financial caregiver can help you avoid otherwise preventable problems, including missed utility, insurance, rent, or mortgage payments.

The financial caregiver cannot sign your checks but can prepare them for your signature. He or she can also help you organize your financial records and make sure your taxes are paid on time.

The financial caregiver may alert you to potential fraud.

The financial caregiver may help identify benefits for which you may be eligible.

Not all illnesses are chronic. An acute illness, regardless if it involves a hospital stay, may make you temporarily unable to take care of your finances. A financial caregiver can step in and take a more active role on a temporary basis.

At your direction, the financial caregiver may establish a relationship with your bank and other professionals. Exercise caution and ask someone you trust to confirm that you have an appropriate set of checks and balances in place to keep your finances simplified, transparent, organized, and protected.

WHO TO CHOOSE?

A good financial caregiver will be younger than you are, in good health, trustworthy, alert, and competent in handling their own financial affairs. Good candidates include:

- Adult children
- Younger siblings
- A close friend

Remember, it is an informal relationship, so you can change financial caregivers at any time. If you have backup caregivers, you can even shift the bulk of the authority from one to another as circumstances or experiences dictate.

Poor candidates include:

- Anyone who intimidates you or makes you feel uneasy

- Someone with known addiction or legal problems

Some seniors consider making financial caregivers out of their health caregivers or household help, but this is a bad idea for several reasons. Such temporary workers are unlikely to have the financial sophistication you need to supervise your investments. They will want to be paid and could become resentful—and even steal from you—if they feel they are not paid enough. They are far more likely to take advantage of you, and far less likely to have your best long-term interests at heart than a trusted friend or family member would. Yes, family members are often prime suspects for financial abuse, but if you have your STOP strategy in place, you can be reasonably secure. You will be far more secure in trusting your finances to someone you know very well as opposed to someone who is temporary hired help.

WHAT ABOUT A FORMAL RELATIONSHIP?

If you want a "formal" relationship with a financial caregiver, you should contact your attorney to arrange it. It might involve giving your financial caregiver power of attorney to work with your bank. If you are still in good health, you might opt to assign your financial caregiver a "durable power of attorney," which becomes active only when specific criteria are met. Typically, the power to enter into transactions would be granted upon a diagnosis of dementia or some other ailment that prevents a person from handling his own financial affairs.

A formal relationship with a financial caregiver advantageously binds the caregiver to act in his client's best interests under the law, but it is an extra cost and might overlap unnecessarily with your professional or informal circle of advisors. In the end, you should choose the relationship that gives you the most peace of mind that your finances are well guarded.

FINANCIAL CAREGIVERS AND YOUR BENEFITS

Can a financial caregiver manage your Social Security benefits? The answer is no. What about someone who holds your power of attorney or is a trustee? The answer is still no.

If you want a third party to manage your benefits, the Social Security Administration requires you to name a Social

Security Representative Payee. You can find more information at https://www.ssa.gov/payee.

What about Medicare? Medicare premiums can be taken directly from your Social Security check. If you have deferred your Social Security benefits, you can still sign up for a free service, Medicare Easy Pay, which allows for payments to be automatically deducted from your bank account monthly. For more information, go to https://www.medicare.gov/your-medicare-costs/paying-parts-a-and-b/medicare-easy-pay.html. Some plans offer payment via a credit or debit card. You can also request that a third party be billed. Use form CMS-2384 available at https://secure.ssa.gov/apps10/poms/images/Other/G-CMS-2384.pdf. Selecting automatic payment options can make life easier for you and for your financial caregiver.

If you are a veteran and want your financial caregiver to handle your benefits, the Department of Veterans Affairs has a "Fiduciary Program" that allows you to do this. But to protect your interests, the VA requires that you provide medical or legal documentation that such delegation is necessary because of age, injury, or illness. For more information, go to http://benefits.va.gov/fiduciary.

WHAT IS THIRD PARTY NOTIFICATION?

Some businesses, such as utility companies, allow you to notify them if a third party is helping you with transactions with the company. On their websites, companies will describe "Third Party Notification" like this:

Occasionally, you or someone close to you may fall behind in paying a bill. With our Third Party Notification, customers who are ill, away from home for an extended period, or unable to handle their own affairs can designate a third party to receive shut-off notices from us. A third party can be a trusted relative, friend, clergy member or social service agency.

Insurance policies (such as Medicare Supplement policies) often have third party notification protocols in place when premiums are late. In such cases, to avoid a policy lapse, the third party receives notice that the payment is late.

CONCLUSION

As with any important decision, there are risks to using a financial caregiver, but we believe the potential benefits far outweigh the potential risks.

Most of the risks are obvious—the financial caregiver could make decisions with which you disagree, he could prove to be dishonest and cheat you, and choosing one of your adult children over another could cause hurt feelings.

But most risks can be guarded against by having a "backup financial caregiver" and by remembering that the financial caregiver is working alongside you, not replacing you. The key is to appoint a financial caregiver (and a backup) *now*—*before* you find yourself incapable of handling your finances. At that point, the decision will be taken out of your hands by a court.

Most of us will need a financial caregiver at some point. So if you haven't already chosen one, get started today.

WORK WITH A SENIOR-FRIENDLY FINANCIAL INSTITUTION

WORK WITH A SENIOR-FRIENDLY FINANCIAL INSTITUTION

E lsewhere in this book, we discuss the advantages of establishing a good personal relationship with your local bank, savings and loan, or credit union. Savings institutions especially value the business of senior citizens, because seniors, as a group, hold a lot of wealth and are savers. If you shop around, you will find that some financial institutions are more "senior-friendly" than others.

WHAT TO LOOK FOR

You may not find a bank or credit union that provides this full suite of services, but at a minimum, it can be a wish list. Ask your local savings institution if they offer:

- Alerts sent to account holders and financial caregivers when regular bills are due or there is suspicious activity on the account
- Read-only (or "View-only") access for authorized third parties
- Opt-in account controls to limit the amount of cash withdrawals
- Opt-in account controls that limit transactions to a city, county, or state
- Financial management assistance if you are incapacitated
- Powers of attorney (some banks have their own exclusive power of attorney forms)
- Policies to cooperate with law enforcement and Adult Protective Services to prevent elder financial abuse

- Petty cash or convenience accounts accessible by a caregiver but restricted to the benefit of the owner, with no right of survivorship

ACCOUNTS WITH REASONABLE FEES

Financial services have a price tag, but some banks offer basic checking accounts with no monthly mainte-nance fees, no minimum balance requirements, and free ATM service if the machines are operated by your own bank. Other fees can be avoided by simple, competent

ATM WARNINGS

It's a good idea to limit ATM use to your own bank for two reasons. The first is that you don't want to pay the fees another bank or independent ATM provider may charge. The second—and more important—is that you want to avoid the additional security risk associated with independent ATMs. Independent ATMs are at higher risk from "skimmer" attacks, where your card information is electronically stolen, than are bank location ATMs. The independents are less likely to have security cameras and other antifraud protections.

financial management, such as overdraft fees. Banks often offer overdraft protection, but they charge for it. In most cases, you don't need it and should opt out of it.

WHAT TO DO IF YOU MOVE YOUR ACCOUNT

Start by establishing a timeframe for completing the move—it will usually take a little time. Open the new account and take the following steps:

- Review the last three monthly statements on your old account to identify recurring automatic deposits and recurring automatic payments
- Move most of your funds to the new account, but leave enough in your old one to cover any outstanding checks or bills that might come due while you're changing accounts; keep enough money in the old account to avoid monthly maintenance fees
- Be sure to inform any organization that sends you checks on a regular basis—your pension provider, annuity companies, Social Security Administration—that you have switched

accounts, and that future checks should be deposited in your new account

- Likewise, make sure that companies that automatically draft money from your account for recurring bill payments have your new account information

REIMBURSEMENT WITH QUICK-PAY APPLICATIONS

Millennials rarely carry much cash and are very comfortable using Venmo, Square Cash, or similar applications to swap funds with their friends. Boomers are less familiar and less comfortable with these new ways of moving funds between bank accounts, but might find them worth a try. We stress the importance of limiting your risk! Don't associate the Venmo account with your primary bank balance, but instead, tie it to a second account that has a limited balance. You can also limit the amount that can be transferred in a single day to a relatively small amount.

Monitor the old account for a month to determine that you have completed the process successfully—then close the old account and transfer its balance of funds to the new account.

KEEPING A SEPARATE SAVINGS ACCOUNT

A savings account is generally more secure than your checking account. Anyone that you pay by check has access to your routing and account number, and could fraudulently remove funds from your account. Your checking account is further exposed to debit card fraud because your debit card is tied directly to the account.

For these reasons, it is important to limit the amount of funds you have in your checking account and maintain a savings account for larger sums of cash. Typically, the only non-signature access to your savings account will be for transfers to your checking account.

CREDIT CARDS—AN IMPORTANT PART OF YOUR BANKING WORLD

Credit cards are an important financial tool. They can make your finances simpler and more transparent, and save you from having to write so many checks. But we do have a few tips on the effective use of credit cards.

Don't let your card cost you unnecessary fees. Certain vendors—typically small stores, gas stations, and government agencies—will charge you a "Convenience Fee" for using a credit card. That fee will generally outweigh the benefit, even after considering any rewards points that you might earn.

Never leave the "tip" space on a credit card charge slip blank. If you tip in cash, or if tipping is not appropriate, either enter a "0" or a strikethrough, and write the total on the charge slip. You never know when a sketchy vendor could add to your charge.

While you want to keep your finances simple, there can be a downside to closing a credit card account you no longer need. Closing the account could actually hurt your credit score, because you are scored on the average length of time your accounts have been open and on the percentage of your outstanding balance to your available credit. So if you expect to need an optimal credit score in the near future, think twice about closing accounts.

If you're traveling, understand that most credit cards will charge you a foreign currency transaction fee. Your best exchange rate will likely come from a bank ATM that is in the same network as your US bank (going out of network could cost you an additional fee). If you travel a lot, shop for cards that don't charge foreign transaction fees.

DEBIT CARDS AND WHY THEY ARE A PROBLEM

The only benefit to a debit card is that you cannot spend more money that you have in your account. But that benefit comes with significant risks.

First, if a purchase is made with a debit card, the funds are immediately withdrawn from your account. With a credit card, you are still in control of the cash. If a vendor is misbehaving, it is much easier to dispute a charge while you are still in possession of the cash.

Second, certain vendors have practices that, while legal, can cost you plenty. Gas stations can put a hold on your account if you pay at the pump, so go inside and pay at the register. Car rental companies have a practice of running a hard inquiry on your credit if you're using a debit card. Hard inquiries have a negative impact on your credit score.

Third, recurring payments for subscriptions and monthly services on your debit card can be difficult to stop, and small monthly charges can go unnoticed for a long time. Putting subscription charges on a credit card adds an additional step between the vendor and your cash; stopping a charge is easier.

Finally, your timeframe for handling a problem is far better with a credit card than with a debit card. Legally, you have sixty days to dispute a transaction on a credit card, and your liability for fraudulent transactions is limited to $50. With a debit card, your $50 fraud limit only lasts for two days, then jumps to $500. After sixty days, the potential loss is unlimited. Many banks promote a "zero liability" guarantee with their debit cards, but that guarantee is limited by the fine print in their terms of use, so proceed with caution.

WHAT ELSE SHOULD YOU LOOK FOR IN A SENIOR-FRIENDLY BANK

Obviously, you want a bank that meets your particular, individual needs, but here are some things to look for as a senior banking customer (and remember to think ahead to what you might not need now, but might need later).

Almost all office buildings are required to abide by the regulations of the Americans with Disabilities Act, but you might find that the physical features of some offices are better than others. Is your bank, for instance, easy to maneuver on a wheelchair? Is the flooring slip-resistant? Are there handrails in the bathrooms, are the chairs easy to get into and out of, and is it generally quiet or noisy?

When it comes to services, you should learn whether your bank offers special discounts or programs (including seminars and webinars) for seniors, whether it allows automated payments online for routine bills, what sort of protection it offers against fraudulent use of your account, what its regulations are for assigning someone your power of attorney, and so on.

Remember, savings institutions want you as a customer and are competing for your business, so make a wish list of features and services that are most important to you and find a bank or credit union or savings and loan where you will be happy as a long-term customer.

AFTERWORD

I f elder financial abuse were only about money, we would not be as passionate about the topic. But it isn't just about money—it's about how you live the rest of your life, and whether your future will be secure or whether you will live with the fear of financial, physical, mental, and emotional abuse.

You may think that, given your circumstances, it is premature to take the action steps we recommend. You're in good health and feel confident about your abilities. But just remember, *it's always too early, until it's too late.*

Before you put this book down, consider all that is at stake if you fail to implement our preventive program.

When it comes to elder financial abuse there are no "give backs." The money is gone and the damage is done.

Your goal is to STOP elder financial abuse by making your finances:

Simple

Transparent

Organized

Protected

Don't be the "easy victim" the perpetrators all look for. Take the offensive!

Your future is in your hands.

ACKNOWLEDGEMENTS

The authors would like to thank their friends and associates who assisted with the completion of this book. Special thanks to James Sullivan CPA (a retirement planning specialist who researched the topics presented and worked with the authors throughout the planning and drafting of the text), Keith Gossett (retired English teacher who worked over the sentence structure), Jay Moore (head of marketing for Tarkenton Financial who assisted with graphics and layout), and Edwin Bevens (chief editor for GoSmallBiz.com who added the final overview and polish). Also, a very special thanks to Marji Ross and her team at Regnery Publishing for making this book a reality.

ENDNOTES

INTRODUCTION

1. J. F. Wasik, "The fleecing of America's elderly," *Consumer Digest* (March/April 2000), 78–79.
2. MetLife Mature Market Inst. et al., *The MetLife Study of Elder Financial Abuse: Crimes of Occasion, Desperation, and Predation Against America's Elders* (Virginia Tech: June 2011), http://ltcombudsman.org/uploads/files/issues/mmi-elder-financial-abuse.pdf.

ACTION STEP 1: RECOGNIZE THAT YOU ARE A TARGET

1. "What Is Elder Abuse," Frequently Asked Questions, National Center on Elder Abuse, https://ncea.acl.gov/faq/index.html#faq1.

2. Reshma Kapadia, "Financial Abuse: The Silent Epidemic," *Barron's*, November 12, 2016.

3. Stephen Deane, "Elder Financial Exploitation: Why it is a concern, what regulators are doing about it, and looking ahead," U.S. Securities and Exchange Commission, Office of the Investor Advocate, https://www.sec.gov/files/elder-financial-exploitation.pdf.

4. Marguerite DeLiema & Kendon J. Conrad, "Financial exploitation of older adults," in *Elder abuse: Research, Practice, and Policy*, (XinQi Dong ed., 1st ed. 2017) p. 141, as cited in above source.

ACTION STEP 2: RECOGNIZE POTENTIAL ABUSERS

1. "Elder Financial Exploitation," Get Involved, National Adult Protective Services, http://www.napsa-now.org/policy-advocacy/exploitation.

2. Jilenne Gunther, MSW, JD, "The 2011 Utah Economic Cost of Elder Financial Exploitation," The National Center for Victims of Crime, 2011, p. 11, http://

victimsofcrime.org/docs/default-source/financial-fraud/2011-economic-cost-of-financial-exploitation.pdf?sfvrsn=2.

3. "Common Ways Family Members and Trusted Others Exploit Vulnerable Adults," Get Involved, National Adult Protective Services, http://www.napsa-now.org/policy-advocacy/exploitation.

ACTION STEP 3: ADMIT THAT YOU ARE VULNERABLE (WE ALL ARE)

1. Keith Jacks Gamble, Patricia A. Boyle, Lei, Yu, and David A. Bennett, "Aging and Financial Decision Making," research supported by the National Institute on Aging grant, June 2014, https://pdfs.semanticscholar.org/5a3b/71938678240d669c6504aec3e48d90fb4edc.pdf.

ACTION STEP 5: MAKE YOUR FINANCES TRANSPARENT

1. Consumer Financial Protection Bureau, "Recommendations and report for financial institutions on preventing and responding to elder financial exploitation," March 2016, https://files.consumerfinance.gov/f/201603_cfpb_recommendations-and-report-for-

financial-institutions-on-preventing-and-responding-to-elder-financial-exploitation.pdf, 21–22.

2.   Ibid, 13.

ACTION STEP 6: ORGANIZE YOUR KEY FINANCIAL, MEDICAL, AND LEGAL DOCUMENTS

1.   Kristen L. Triebel, Daniel C. Marson, "The Warning Sings of Diminished Financial Capacity in Older Adults," *Generations* Vol. 36, No. 2 (Summer 2012), https://www.questia.com/library/journal/1P3-2717110131/the-warning-signs-of-diminished-financial-capacity.

ACTION STEP 7: PROTECT YOUR PERSONAL IDENTITY INFORMATION (PIL)

1.   Federal Trade Commission, "Identity Theft: Military Personnel & Families: What to know, What to do," September 2016, https://www.consumer.ftc.gov/articles/pdf-0016_military_idt_what_to_know_what_to_do.pdf.

INDEX

NOTES